How to Buy Your First Home

Ricardo Moreno

Copyright Page

Publisher: Flamenco
Release Year 2025

Index

Defining Your Dream of Owning a Home 7
Financial Mindset 12
Are You Really Ready? 18
Calculating How Much You Can Afford to Spend 24
Saving for a Down Payment Without Sacrificing Your Life 30
Smart Credit 36
Loans and Financing Options Explained 42
The Secret of a Good Investment 48
How to Analyze a Property 53
The Real Estate Agent 59
Strategies to Negotiate Like an Expert 64
The Hidden Costs No One Tells You About 70
From Offer to Contract 76
The Perfect Move 82
Your First Home as an Investment for the Future 87

Defining Your Dream of Owning a Home

Owning a home is one of those dreams that many people share, but few stop to really think about what it means to them. The idea of owning a home is often accompanied by happy images: a family gathered in the dining room, a garden where children play, or simply the feeling of having something that truly belongs to you. However, beyond those pretty images, there's a key question everyone should ask themselves before beginning this process: Why do I want to own a home?

For some people, the reason is emotional. They grew up in a family that always rented, and they feel that owning a home would give them a sense of stability and security they never had. Others see buying a home as a long-term investment, something that will increase in value over time and give them greater financial peace of mind. And there are those who simply dream of personalizing their space, without landlord restrictions or temporary contracts. No matter your reason, the key is to keep it clear and realistic, because that reason will drive you throughout the entire process, even when you face obstacles.

Defining your dream home also involves visualizing what you want your life to be like in that house. Is it a large house with a garden, or would you prefer a smaller, well-located apartment? Do you imagine it in a vibrant city or in the suburbs, surrounded by tranquility? Thinking about these details isn't wasting time; it's shaping your goal. The clearer you are about what type of home fits your lifestyle and future plans, the easier it will be to make smart decisions later on.

Another crucial point is to understand that buying a home is more than just buying bricks and mortar. It's about committing to a community, a location, and a lifestyle. Do you want to be close to your family? Do you prefer to live close to work to avoid long hours in traffic? Are you interested in having nearby schools for your children or supermarkets and transportation close by? Defining these aspects will save you the frustration of ending up in a place that doesn't fit your needs.

Additionally, it's important to be honest with yourself about your priorities and limitations.

You may dream of a huge house, but if it means living in debt for the next 30 years, is it worth it? This is where the emotional aspect must be balanced with logic. Your dream should be something that motivates you, but it should also be achievable. Owning a home shouldn't become a financial burden that robs you of your peace of mind. It's better to start with something more modest that you can afford and improve over time than to try to achieve something beyond your capabilities just because it sounds more impressive.

Finally, remember that this dream is yours and no one else's. Sometimes, the expectations of family, friends, or society push us to pursue something that doesn't actually make us happy. It's easy to get caught up in the idea that you should have a house of a certain size or in a certain location because "that's how it's supposed to be." But at the end of the day, you're the one who will live there, who will pay the mortgage, and who will enjoy—or suffer—the consequences of that decision. Make sure your dream of owning a home is authentically yours, based on your desires, your needs, and your reality.

Defining your dream of owning a home isn't just about imagining what the house will look like, but also about understanding why you want it and how it fits into your long-term life. It's the first step, but one of the most important, because it will give you the clarity and motivation to keep going when the process gets complicated. And believe me, it will eventually. But if you know exactly why you want that home, it will be much easier to stay focused and move forward until you achieve it.

Financial Mindset

Buying your first home isn't just a question of money; it's also a question of mindset. The way you think about money, your financial habits, and your daily priorities play a huge role in determining whether you'll achieve your goal or not. Most people view buying a home as a huge expense, but the truth is, it's an investment, and to make a good investment, you need to think like an investor, not a spender.

First, it's vital to understand that owning a home is very different from renting. When you rent, you only think about the monthly payment and not breaking anything so the landlord doesn't overcharge you. Owning a home, on the other hand, means being responsible for everything: mortgage payments, maintenance, taxes, utilities, and any unforeseen events that arise. That's not a bad thing, but it does require a more organized and forward-thinking mindset. It's not just about being able to buy the home, but about being able to maintain it without it overwhelming you financially.

To begin building this mindset, it's crucial to stop thinking of money as something that simply comes in and goes out each month. Many people live with the idea that as long as they have enough to cover their expenses and treat themselves, everything is fine. But to buy a home, you need to view your money as a tool to build something bigger. Every financial decision you make should move you closer or further away from your goal of homeownership. Small, seemingly harmless expenses, like eating out every day or buying unnecessary things, become silent obstacles that delay your dream.

A key mindset shift is to start prioritizing building wealth. Every time you pay rent, that money is gone forever, leaving you nothing in return. On the other hand, when you pay the mortgage on your own home, that money builds something that belongs to you and will increase in value over time. It's like the difference between leasing a car and owning one: at the end of the lease, you're left with nothing. With a home, at the end of the mortgage, you have a valuable asset.

This doesn't mean you should stop enjoying life while you save, but it does mean you should be more conscious and selective with your spending. For example, if you spend $30 every time you go out to dinner and you do it three times a week, that's almost $4,000 a year that you could have put toward your down payment. Is that dinner worth it, or would you rather have your house sooner? It's not about living with extreme restrictions, but rather understanding that every expense is a choice that affects your goals.

Additionally, it's essential to start thinking long-term. Many people only focus on the monthly mortgage payment and forget that the home will also have other costs. You'll need money for repairs, improvements, and even emergencies. Having a homeowner's financial mindset means planning beyond the basic numbers and creating a financial cushion to protect yourself from unexpected events. No one wants to end up buying a home only to lose it because they couldn't afford to maintain it.

Another key point is to let go of the instant gratification mentality. We live in an age where we want everything fast: food, shopping, answers. But buying a home requires patience. Saving for a down payment can take time, improving your credit can take time, and finding the right home doesn't happen overnight. This is where a strong mindset comes into play: you need to stay grounded and constantly remind yourself that the effort will be worth it.

Finally, it's important to see yourself as someone capable of owning a home. It may sound strange, but many people fail because, deep down, they don't believe they can actually achieve it. If you've always seen yourself as someone who "can only rent" or who "will never be able to save enough," your mind will work against you without you even realizing it. The right financial mindset includes changing not only your habits but also your beliefs. You have to start seeing yourself as someone who deserves and can own their own home, because when you truly believe this, your actions will begin to align with that vision.

Adopting this new mindset doesn't happen overnight, but every small change counts.

Every time you choose to save instead of spending impulsively, every time you plan your finances instead of winging it, and every time you remember your long-term goal instead of focusing only on the present, you're taking one step closer to your new home.

Are You Really Ready?

Buying a home is one of the biggest and most exciting decisions you can make, but it's also one of the most serious. It's easy to get carried away with the idea of owning a place and start imagining the decor, family gatherings, or the peace of mind that comes with not having to deal with a landlord. However, before jumping in headfirst, it's crucial to ask yourself an honest question: Are you really ready to take this step? And it's not just a matter of whether you have enough money, but whether you're emotionally, financially, and practically ready to take on what homeownership means.

The first thing you should assess is your current financial situation. Having a general idea of your income and expenses isn't enough. You need to know exactly how much money comes in and out each month. Do you have outstanding debts? How much are you saving? Is your job stable or does your income fluctuate? Buying a home means committing to making monthly payments for many years, and you can't rely solely on the hope that everything will stay the same or improve over time. You must be realistic and ask yourself if you could continue paying the mortgage if something unexpected happened, such as losing your job or having a medical emergency. If the answer is no, perhaps it's not the time yet.

In addition to the monthly mortgage payment, there are other important expenses you can't overlook. Many people make the mistake of thinking only about the price of the home and forgetting about additional costs. Taxes, insurance, maintenance, utilities, and potential repairs are expenses that can add up to much more than you imagined. Therefore, it's essential to crunch the numbers beyond the monthly payment and make sure you can manage the entire package without coming up short each month.

Another key point is your emergency fund. Having only enough saved for the down payment and closing costs is a dangerous strategy. Life is full of surprises, and owning a home means any problems are your responsibility. If the water heater breaks or the roof starts leaking, you can't call the landlord because you're now the owner. Before buying, you should have an extra fund equal to at least three to six months of your fixed expenses. This will give you peace of mind knowing that, no matter what happens, you'll be able to keep your home without going into debt or losing it.

But being ready isn't just a matter of money. It's also important to ask yourself if you're emotionally ready for the commitment that homeownership entails. Owning a home isn't just about having a place to live; it's about having a long-term responsibility. You'll no longer be able to easily move if you don't like something or if you get a job offer in another city. You also won't be able to call your landlord to fix things when something breaks. You'll have to accept that, from now on, you'll be responsible for everything that happens in your home, from repairs to the daily care of the property.

It's also essential to think about your current lifestyle and how it will change with homeownership. Do you travel frequently? Do you prefer fewer responsibilities and more freedom to move around? Owning your own home can be wonderful, but it can also limit you in some ways. If you feel like you haven't found the place you want to settle down in for several years or are worried about being tied to one location, it may be better to wait a little longer. Buying a home is easier than selling one, and you don't want to end up in a situation where you feel trapped.

Finally, assess your true motivations. Sometimes, the desire to buy a home comes more from social or family pressure than from your own well-thought-out desire. Maybe your friends have already bought their homes, or your parents insist you stop renting because "it's a waste of money." It's easy to be influenced, but the reality is that no one else is going to pay your mortgage or live with the consequences of your decision. Make sure you're buying a home because it's what you truly want and because it fits with your life plans, not because you feel it's what's expected of you.

Being truly ready to buy your first home doesn't mean having everything figured out 100 percent, but it does mean being clear about your finances, your emotional situation, and your future plans. If after analyzing all these points you're still convinced you want to take the plunge, then you're on the right track. And if you find you're not ready yet, don't worry. It's better to wait and prepare well than to jump in unsure and end up with a burden you can't handle. The right home will be waiting for you when you're ready for it.

Calculating How Much You Can Afford to Spend

One of the most common mistakes when looking to buy a home is falling in love with a property without first knowing how much you can actually afford to spend. It's easy to get carried away with excitement, see a perfect house, and start imagining what it would be like to live there. But if you don't run the numbers first, that dream can turn into a financial nightmare. Knowing exactly how much you can spend isn't just a matter of how much you earn, but also how your overall finances look and how comfortably you'll be able to afford the home without sacrificing your quality of life.

The first step is to understand your net monthly income, that is, the money you actually receive after taxes and deductions. This is the base number you'll work with. From there, you need to calculate your current fixed expenses: rent, food, transportation, utilities, subscriptions, debt, and any other essential expenses month after month. Don't leave anything out, because the goal here is to have a clear picture of how much money you have left after covering all the basics.

A general rule of thumb used by many experts is the 28/36 rule. This means you shouldn't spend more than 28 percent of your gross monthly income (before taxes) on total housing costs, including your mortgage, taxes, home insurance, and utilities. Furthermore, your total debt—including credit cards, car loans, student loans, and any other type of debt—shouldn't exceed 36 percent of your gross income. This formula is a solid guideline to ensure you don't end up living just to pay for your house.

For example, if you earn $3,000 a month before taxes, 28 percent would be $840. That means your monthly mortgage payment, plus taxes and home insurance, shouldn't exceed that amount. If you already have other debts, such as a car loan or credit card, those payments along with the mortgage shouldn't exceed $1,080 (36 percent of your income). It's a simple but effective formula to ensure you're not getting into a house that, even if it looks perfect, will be impossible to maintain in the long term.

However, general rules are just the beginning. It's important to go further and think about your lifestyle and future plans. Do you want to continue going out on the weekends? Do you plan to have children soon? Would you like to travel every year? These are expenses that aren't always reflected in the formulas, but they will impact your ability to afford a house without feeling like you're financially drowning. It's no use having a nice house if you can't enjoy life because all your money is going toward the mortgage.

Another point many people forget is the emergency fund. Owning a home means surprises are inevitable. An appliance that stops working, a burst pipe, or even an unexpected increase in property taxes can throw your budget out of whack if you don't have a financial cushion. Before deciding how much you can afford to spend on a home, make sure you can also continue to feed your emergency fund. Ideally, you should have at least three to six months of your essential expenses set aside to cover any unexpected events without going into debt.

Then there's the issue of the down payment. The more money you can put down, the lower your monthly mortgage will be and the less interest you'll pay over the long term. Most lenders require at least 10 percent of the home's value as a down payment, but if you can get to 20 percent, you'll avoid private mortgage insurance, which is an additional cost that protects the bank, not you. For example, if the house you like costs $200,000, you'd need at least $20,000 down to avoid that extra insurance. It's a lot of money, yes, but in the long run, it can save you thousands of dollars.

Finally, it's vital to be honest with yourself. It's tempting to stretch yourself to the limit to achieve the house that seems perfect, but living on the edge of your budget will leave you with no room to enjoy life or deal with unexpected events. Buying a home should give you peace of mind and satisfaction, not anxiety about making ends meet. It's better to start with a more modest home that you can comfortably afford and improve over time, than to jump into something out of reach just because of appearance or social pressure.

Calculating how much you can afford to spend isn't the most exciting step in this process, but it's one of the most important. It's the difference between having a home you're happy with and one that becomes a burden. Knowing your numbers, being realistic, and planning wisely will give you the confidence that when you finally put the keys in the lock of your new house, you'll know that you not only chose the right place, but that you did so in a way that protects your well-being and your future.

Saving for a Down Payment Without Sacrificing Your Life

Saving for a down payment on your first home can feel like an impossible mountain to climb, especially when you look at home prices and do the quick math. The amount you need to come up with can seem overwhelming, and the idea of sacrificing your life for years just to scrape that money together can be demotivating. But here's the truth that few people tell you: yes, saving for a down payment is essential, but you don't have to put your life on hold to achieve it. The key is to find a smart balance between your goals and your daily life, and to understand that every dollar you save now is a direct investment in your future.

The first thing you need to be clear about is how much you really need. Most lenders suggest a down payment of 20 percent of the home's price to avoid paying private mortgage insurance, but that doesn't mean it's the only option. There are programs that accept lower down payments, even as low as 3 or 5 percent. For example, if the home you're interested in costs $200,000, 20 percent would be $40,000, while 5 percent would be only $10,000. The difference is huge, and while putting more money down saves you on interest and insurance, not everyone can afford that amount right away. The important thing is to know your exact goal, because saving without a clear number is like running a marathon without knowing where the finish line is.

Once you know how much you need, the next step is to design a plan that's realistic and sustainable. The most common mistake is thinking that saving means cutting out all the pleasures in your life. It's not about living on a shoestring or giving up on every little joy. That only leads to frustration and, sooner or later, giving up on saving. Instead, the smart strategy is to identify expenses that don't contribute much to your true happiness and redirect that money toward your down payment. For example, subscriptions you don't use, eating out out of habit rather than pleasure, or impulse purchases that end up forgotten in a drawer. You don't need to eliminate all your luxuries, but you do need to be aware of which ones you truly enjoy and which ones are just pointless habits.

It's also helpful to change your mindset about saving. Instead of seeing it as a deprivation, see it as an investment in your future freedom. Every dollar you save brings you closer to the home you want and reduces the amount you'll pay in interest for years to come. For example, if you manage to save $5,000 more than planned, you'll not only have a lower monthly payment, but you could save thousands in interest over the life of your mortgage. Every small sacrifice now translates into a big reward later.

A practical way to accelerate your savings without feeling like you're giving up everything is to automate the process. Set up an automatic transfer to a separate account dedicated solely to the down payment, right when you receive your paycheck. That way, you pay yourself first, and the money doesn't get mixed up with your daily expenses. It's easier not to spend what you never see. Plus, having a specific account for the down payment creates a psychological barrier: you'll have a harder time touching that money because you know it has an important purpose.

Another strategy many people overlook is looking for ways to increase their income, not just cutting expenses. This doesn't mean working yourself to exhaustion, but it does mean being creative. Do you have any skills you could monetize on the weekends? Can you sell things you no longer use? Is there a way to earn extra money from home? Sometimes, earning a little extra is more effective and less painful than trying to cut every last cent from your expenses.

It's also important to celebrate your progress, no matter how small. Saving for a down payment can feel like a long and lonely process, so recognizing your accomplishments keeps you motivated. If you manage to save more than planned one month, give yourself a small reward that won't derail your progress. The key is to find the motivation to keep going without feeling like your life revolves solely around saving.

Finally, remember that patience is part of the process. Saving for a down payment on a house isn't something that happens overnight, and it's okay for it to take time. The goal isn't just to save the money, but to approach your home purchase feeling stable and prepared, not exhausted and resentful of the sacrifices you've made.

Saving for a down payment without sacrificing your life is entirely possible. It's all about having a clear strategy, being mindful of your expenses, finding ways to increase your income, and staying motivated. When you finally have the keys in hand and step into your own home for the first time, every effort will have been worth it. Your house will be much more than four walls; it will be the result of your determination and your ability to balance your dreams with your daily life. And that, more than the money you save, will be what you'll be most proud of.

Smart Credit

When it comes to buying your first home, credit is one of those topics that most people underestimate or don't fully understand until it's too late. Having smart credit doesn't just mean having a credit card and paying it on time. It's much more than that. It's building a financial reputation that tells banks and lenders that you're a safe bet, someone they can lend a large amount of money to with the confidence that you'll pay it back. And the reality is, the better your credit history, the easier it will be to get a mortgage, with better terms and lower interest rates.

First, it's vital to understand what a credit score is and how it's calculated. Basically, it's a number that reflects how reliable you are at repaying debts. This score is based on several factors: your payment history, your total debt, how long you've had credit, what type of credit you have, and how many recent credit applications you've made. Banks use this number to decide whether to approve you for a mortgage and what interest rate to offer you. The higher your score, the better your terms, and that can mean saving thousands of dollars over the life of your loan.

If your credit isn't in the best shape, don't panic. It doesn't mean you'll never be able to buy a home, but it does mean you'll have to work on improving it before applying for a mortgage. The good news is that improving your credit isn't as complicated as it seems, although it does require discipline and time. The first step is checking your credit history. Many people don't even know what their score is or if they have errors on their report that are hurting them. Errors are more common than you think: misreported payments, accounts you don't recognize, or debts you've already paid that keep appearing. Correcting these errors can give your score a quick boost.

Once you've established your credit history, the next step is to make sure you pay all your debts on time. This is the most important factor for your credit score. A single late payment can damage your score and remain there for years. If you're someone who forgets payment dates, set up automatic reminders or, better yet, activate automatic payments. This eliminates the risk of forgetting and ensures your payment history remains spotless.

Another key point is your debt level. Banks don't just look at whether you pay on time; they also want to see how much debt you have compared to the credit you have available. If your credit cards are always maxed out, that raises a red flag, even if you make payments on time. The general rule is to keep your credit utilization below 30 percent of your total limit. For example, if you have a card with a $5,000 limit, try not to owe more than $1,500. The lower that ratio, the better for your score.

If you don't have much of a credit history, it might seem like a good thing because you haven't accumulated debt, but lenders actually prefer to see that you have experience managing credit responsibly. One way to start is to open a small credit card, use it for basic expenses, and pay it off each month. You can also ask to be an authorized user on the card of a family member with good credit. This adds their positive history to yours and helps you build credit faster.

On the other hand, it's important to avoid the temptation to open multiple credit accounts at once. Every time you apply for a new card or loan, it creates a hard inquiry on your credit history, and too many of these inquiries in a short period of time can lower your score. Lenders might see this as a sign that you're desperate for credit or planning to take on more debt than you can handle.

When your credit is finally in good shape and you're ready to apply for a mortgage, be sure to compare offers from different banks or lenders. Don't settle for the first option offered. Although all mortgages seem similar at first glance, small differences in interest rates or closing costs can make a big difference in the total amount you'll pay over the long term. Smart credit also means being a smart shopper.

Credit isn't something you build overnight, but every effort you make now will pay off when it's time to look for a home. Having strong credit will not only allow you to access a mortgage, but it will also open the door to better terms, lower rates, and more manageable monthly payments. And that, at the end of the day, means less stress and more money in your pocket to enjoy your new life as a homeowner. Smart credit isn't just a number; it's a tool that brings you closer to your dream of owning a home, and the more you take care of that tool, the easier it will be to achieve it.

Loans and Financing Options Explained

When it comes time to buy your first home, you likely don't have all the money saved up to pay for it upfront. That's where loans and financing options come in. They're basically a way for the bank to lend you the money you need so you can buy the house now and pay for it little by little over time. However, not all loans are created equal, and choosing the right one can make a big difference in how much you end up paying in the end. That's why understanding your options is key to making a smart decision.

First, let's talk about the traditional mortgage. It's the most common type of home loan. It generally comes in two main formats: fixed-rate and adjustable-rate. A fixed-rate mortgage means the interest you pay each month will be the same for the life of the loan, whether it's 15, 20, or 30 years. It's a popular option because it gives you stability and predictability. You know exactly how much you'll pay each month, which makes it easier to manage your budget. On the other hand, there's an adjustable-rate mortgage, where the interest can change after a certain period of time. For example, you could have a fixed rate for the first five years, but after that, it adjusts annually based on market rates. The advantage of this option is that the initial rate is usually lower than a fixed mortgage, but you have to be careful because if rates rise, your monthly payment will also rise. This option can be attractive if you plan to sell your home or refinance before the rate begins to adjust.

Another option is government-backed loans. These are ideal for first-time buyers who don't have perfect credit or can't come up with a large down payment. The most well-known is the FHA loan, backed by the Federal Housing Administration. It allows down payments as low as 3.5 percent and has more flexible credit requirements than traditional mortgages. The downside is that it requires paying additional mortgage insurance, which increases your monthly payment, but it's still a great option for those who don't have large savings or need more flexibility to qualify.

There's also the VA loan, designed for veterans and active members of the armed forces. This type of financing is incredibly beneficial because it allows you to purchase a home with no down payment and no mortgage insurance, which can save you thousands of dollars. If you qualify, it's hard to find a better option than this.

Then there's the USDA loan, aimed at those buying in rural or suburban areas. It offers the option of buying with no down payment, but there are income limits and the property must be in an eligible area. It's an excellent option if you're looking to live outside of large cities and qualify for the program.

One option some people consider is direct seller financing. In this case, the homeowner acts as the lender. Basically, you reach an agreement with them to pay for the house in installments, without going through a bank. This option can be helpful if you're having trouble qualifying for a traditional mortgage, but you need to be very careful with the terms. It's crucial to make sure the contract is clear, legal, and doesn't leave you vulnerable if something goes wrong.

Regardless of which option you're interested in, it's essential to understand how interest rates and loan terms work. The longer the term, the lower your monthly payments will be, but the more interest you'll pay over the long term. For example, on a 30-year loan, your monthly payment will be lower than on a 15-year loan, but you'll end up paying significantly more in interest over the life of the loan. On the other hand, a 15-year loan allows you to own a home much faster and pay less interest, but your monthly payments will be higher. The key is finding the balance that works for you and your financial situation.

Furthermore, the type of loan isn't everything. Closing costs are also an important part of financing. These include things like lender fees, the home appraisal, taxes, and insurance. They're typically between 2 and 5 percent of the home's price, so don't underestimate them. Some loans allow you to include these costs in the financed amount, but that means you'll end up paying interest on them as well. It's best to try to cover these expenses out of pocket if possible.

At the end of the day, choosing the right loan isn't just a matter of numbers. It's a decision that affects your daily life for years. A monthly payment that's too high can make your house feel more like a burden than a home, while a loan with a low rate and manageable payments can give you peace of mind and stability. Take the time to research, compare, and ask questions. Banks will want to sell you what's right for them, but you have to find what's right for you. Understanding your financing options is one of the most important decisions you'll make along this journey, and doing it wisely can be the difference between a stress-filled experience and a purchase you'll enjoy and feel proud of every time you walk through the door of your new home.

The Secret of a Good Investment

When you buy your first home, it's easy to get carried away by the excitement and think only about how the decorated living room will look or how big the garden will be. But beyond the excitement, there's something crucial that can't be overlooked: a home isn't just a place to live; it's also an investment. And like any investment, there are decisions that can make it a great one or turn it into a financial headache. The secret to a good real estate investment isn't finding the prettiest house, but choosing a property that will appreciate in value over time and leave you better off financially, not worse off.

To begin with, you need to understand that the value of a home doesn't just depend on the home itself. It depends on where it's located. Location is, without a doubt, the most important factor in real estate investing. An average home in a good neighborhood will always be worth more than a spectacular home in a rundown or underdeveloped area. But what makes a good location? There are several clues you can follow. Look for neighborhoods that are growing, where new shops, schools, or transportation hubs are being built. Places with good connectivity, security, and amenities will always be more attractive. Even if the area doesn't look perfect today, if there are signs of growth, the property's value is likely to increase over the years.

Another key aspect is the purchase price. A good investment starts when you buy the house, not when you sell it. That means you need to make sure you're not paying more than it's actually worth. People often fall in love with a property and end up offering more money just to beat other buyers. That's a costly mistake. The idea isn't to beat everyone else; it's to get the best possible house at the best possible price. To do that, research the prices of similar homes in the same area and use that information to negotiate. If you buy a home below market value or at a good price in a growing area, you're already halfway there.

It's also important to consider the home's potential. Don't just focus on how it looks now, but also on what it could be. Sometimes, a home with an old kitchen or a shabby exterior scares off other buyers and sells for less. But if the problems are cosmetic rather than structural, a small investment in remodeling can significantly increase its value. Painting, updating the kitchen, or improving the garden can give a huge boost to the home's value if you decide to sell it in the future.

Of course, it's not all about looks. A good investment also means making sure the home is in good condition. You don't want to end up buying something that looks good on the outside but is riddled with hidden problems. It's essential to do a full inspection of the property before closing the deal. Check the structure, electrical wiring, plumbing, and roof. Major and expensive repairs can wipe out any potential profit you were hoping for.

Also, don't forget the extra expenses that come with owning a home. Taxes, maintenance, utilities, and repairs are all part of the equation. A cheaper home with sky-high taxes or one that requires constant repairs can end up costing you more than a more expensive home in better condition.

Finally, think about your future. A home that's a good investment today should still be a good investment in a few years. Will the area continue to grow, or is it likely to decline? Does the home have room for your family to grow if you plan to stay long-term? Could you easily rent it out if you decide to move? These are questions worth asking before you commit.

The secret to a good real estate investment isn't luck, it's preparation. It's about research, analysis, and thinking beyond the emotion of the moment. If you choose well, you'll not only have a home to live in, but also an asset that will increase your wealth and give you financial stability in the future. Buying a home isn't just an emotional decision; it's a smart strategy when done right.

How to Analyze a Property

Choosing the perfect home goes far beyond whether it looks beautiful or has the garden you've always dreamed of. To ensure you're truly making the right decision, it's essential to analyze the property in detail and strategically. Every home has secrets that aren't readily apparent, and knowing these details will help you determine whether it's a good buy or a trap disguised as an opportunity.

The first thing you should consider is the location. It doesn't matter how perfect the house is on the inside if it's in an area where no one wants to live or where property values aren't rising. Consider how close basic services like supermarkets, schools, hospitals, and public transportation are. A convenient location not only makes your life easier, but also ensures that the house will be attractive to future buyers or tenants if you ever decide to sell or rent it.

Next, study the neighborhood. Walk around the area at different times of the day to observe the atmosphere. Is it quiet and safe, or is there constant noise and a lot of suspicious activity? A place may seem ideal in the morning, but completely transform by nightfall. Also, look at the overall condition of the other homes. If most are well-maintained, that's a good sign that neighbors care about the area, and the neighborhood is less likely to decline over time.

Once you're satisfied with the location, it's time to analyze the house's structure. Appearance is important, but what really counts is the solidity of the construction. A house with structural problems can become a bottomless pit of expenses. Pay attention to the walls, ceilings, and floors. Look for large cracks, damp patches, or areas where the paint is peeling, as these are often signs of deeper problems. Open and close doors and windows to make sure they aren't warped or difficult to move, as this may indicate that the structure has shifted over time.

Also check the roof. It's one of the most expensive parts to repair, so it's vital that it's in good condition. If you see broken shingles, water stains, or sagging areas, that could indicate leaks or significant damage. A professional inspection is a good investment here, because roof problems aren't always visible from below.

The electrical system is another key point. Make sure there are enough outlets in each room and that the electrical box is modern and safe. Older systems can be dangerous and can't handle the power consumption of today's appliances. Turning on lights, testing outlets, and verifying that everything is working properly can save you from unpleasant surprises after you move out.

As for plumbing, turn on the faucets and check the water pressure. A weak stream can be a sign of old pipes or hidden problems. Also, inspect the bathrooms and kitchen to make sure there are no leaks or unpleasant odors. Plumbing repairs can be expensive and complicated, so it's better to be safe than sorry.

Don't forget about outdoor space. A beautiful garden is nice, but it's also extra work. Think about how much time and money you're willing to invest in maintaining it. Also, check the drainage. A property that floods every time it rains can be a nightmare.

Another point many overlook is the home's history. Ask how long it's been on the market. If it hasn't sold for too long, that could be a sign that something is wrong. It's also helpful to find out why the current owners are selling. Sometimes the reasons are personal, but other times they may be running away from a problem they don't want to face.

Finally, take a close look at the price. Compare the property to similar properties in the area. If the price is well below average, it could be a bargain, but there may also be hidden problems. And if the price is too high, you may be paying more for the neighborhood's name than for the house itself.

Analyzing a property takes time and effort, but it's worth it. Don't get caught up in the excitement of imagining how it will look furnished or how beautiful your life will be there. A home is a long-term investment, and taking the time to thoroughly research it will give you the peace of mind that comes from knowing you're making a smart, informed decision. Remember that the perfect home doesn't just feel right; it must also make financial and structural sense. If you overlook any of these points, you could end up stuck with a property that gives you more headaches than joy. But if you do your homework, you'll find not only a beautiful house, but a solid home and a smart investment for your future.

The Real Estate Agent

When you decide to buy your first home, one of the first dilemmas you'll face is whether to work with a real estate agent or go it alone. Some people think they can save money by avoiding agents, while others find having a professional on their side makes the process easier. The reality is that a real estate agent can be a great ally if you choose the right person, but they can also become a hindrance if you don't choose well. Therefore, it's essential to understand their role and how to ensure they're truly working in your best interest.

A good real estate agent is much more than just someone who shows you houses. Their job is to help you find the best property within your budget, negotiate the best possible price, and guide you through all the purchasing procedures. They can also offer valuable market information, explain the documents you'll be signing, and help you avoid costly mistakes. However, not all agents are the same. Some focus on selling quickly without considering your true value, while others take the time to find the best fit for you.

To choose a good real estate agent, the first step is to do your research. Don't settle for the first one you find or one recommended by a friend without first doing your own evaluation. Ask how many years of experience they have, what areas they work in, and how many homes they've sold recently. An experienced agent knows the market well and knows how to identify opportunities you might not see. It's also important to have good references. If other buyers have had positive experiences with them, they're more likely to do a good job for you.

Another key aspect is communication. A good real estate agent should listen to you and understand exactly what you're looking for. If they show you homes from the start that don't meet your criteria or pressure you to buy quickly, it's a red flag. You don't need someone who just wants to close a sale, but someone who truly cares about finding the right home for you. Patience is a good indicator that the agent is more interested in your satisfaction than their commission.

It's also important to understand how real estate agents are paid. In most cases, their commission is paid by the property seller, meaning you, as the buyer, won't be paid directly. However, this also means that some agents may be more motivated to sell specific properties that generate a higher commission, rather than focusing on what's truly in your best interest. Ask from the outset how they handle their commission and make sure their interests align with yours.

A common misconception is that you only need one agent for the entire process. If you don't feel comfortable with the person you choose, you can change them at any time. You're not obligated to stay with an agent who isn't meeting your expectations. Make sure you understand any clauses that require you to work only with that person for a specific period before signing any agreement.

If you decide not to work with an agent, be prepared to take on many of their duties. You'll have to search for properties yourself, contact sellers, schedule showings, negotiate the price, and handle all the paperwork. This can be advantageous if you're meticulous and like to have complete control of the process, but it can also be exhausting if you're inexperienced in real estate. A good compromise is to use an agent only for the more complicated parts, such as negotiation and closing, but do the initial property search yourself.

Ultimately, the real estate agent's role is to help you make an informed decision and make the process easier for you. If you choose well, you'll have someone who will save you time, money, and stress. But if you choose poorly, you could end up with a house you're not happy with or paying more than you should. Don't be afraid to ask questions, do your research, and, above all, trust your intuition. A good real estate agent doesn't just sell houses; they also build trusting relationships with their clients. And when it comes to the most important purchase of your life, that's what you really need.

Strategies to Negotiate Like an Expert

Negotiating the price of a home can seem intimidating, especially if it's your first time, but the reality is that everything in real estate is negotiable. The difference between paying full price or getting a good discount depends on your preparation, your strategy, and your confidence in the process. Buying a home isn't like buying a product at a store with a fixed price. Here, the number you see in the initial offer is just the starting point, and the true price is determined during the negotiation.

The first thing you should do is do your research. Before making any offer, analyze the market. Compare the price of the house with other similar properties in the area. If you find that other properties with similar characteristics are selling for less, you have a solid negotiating argument. Also, find out how long the house has been on the market. If it's been on the market for months without selling, it's a sign that the seller might be willing to lower the price to close the deal.

Another key to negotiating well is understanding the seller's motivation. Not all homeowners sell for the same reasons.

Some need to sell quickly because they're moving to another city, others are in financial trouble and looking for cash, and some are simply trying their luck to get a good deal. If you can figure out why the owner is selling, you can use that information to your advantage. A desperate seller is much more open to negotiating than one who isn't in a hurry.

When it comes time to make your offer, don't make the mistake of offering the highest price right from the start. Start with a lower, but still reasonable, figure. If the list price is $200,000, don't offer $120,000 because the seller probably won't even take you seriously. But if you offer $180,000 with a clear justification based on the property's condition or local prices, you could start a favorable negotiation.

A very useful psychological trick is to avoid showing too much enthusiasm. If the seller senses you're too excited about the house, they'll assume you're willing to pay anything for it and will be less flexible in the negotiation. Maintain a neutral attitude, ask questions about the property's defects, and make it clear you have other options in mind. When the seller feels you could walk away at any moment, they're more willing to lower the price to ensure you close the deal.

Another key aspect is negotiating beyond price. Sometimes the seller doesn't want to lower the price because they have a specific number in mind, but that doesn't mean you can't get other benefits. You can ask them to include appliances, furniture, or cover part of the closing costs. You can even negotiate to have certain repairs made before the sale. In the long run, these concessions can save you thousands of dollars, even if the purchase price doesn't drop as much as you'd like.

Knowing when to stay silent is also a powerful tool. During negotiations, many people feel the need to fill the silence with words, but sometimes it's better to let the seller do the talking. When you make an offer and remain silent, you put pressure on the other party to respond. In many cases, the seller will try to justify their price or make a lower counteroffer than they had planned.

Also, never be afraid to walk away. The best weapon in any negotiation is being willing to walk away if the deal isn't fair. If the seller sees you're not desperate, they're more likely to come back with a better offer. Often, buyers make the mistake of falling in love with a house and feeling that if they don't buy it, they'll miss out on the opportunity of a lifetime. The truth is, there are always more houses available, and if you stick with it, you'll find one that fits your budget and needs without compromising your financial stability.

Finally, consider having a real estate agent negotiate for you. If you have a good agent on your side, they'll already have experience in these types of negotiations and know how to handle seller tactics. However, don't leave everything in their hands. Make sure they're truly fighting for your interests and not just trying to close the sale as quickly as possible.

Negotiating is an art that is learned with practice and preparation. It's not about winning or losing, but rather finding a middle ground where both parties feel comfortable with the agreement. If you follow these strategies and stand firm in your position, you'll increase your chances of getting the house you want at the best possible price. Remember that in real estate, what you don't negotiate is what you end up paying.

The Hidden Costs No One Tells You About

When buying a home for the first time, most people focus solely on the purchase price and the monthly mortgage payment. However, there's a long list of hidden costs that can surprise you if you don't consider them from the start. These additional expenses can make the process more expensive than you imagined and, in some cases, can seriously affect your budget if you're not prepared.

One of the most unexpected costs is paying property taxes. In some locations, annual taxes can represent a significant amount of money, and in many cases, the buyer must pay a portion of these taxes upfront at closing. Depending on the home's location and value, you could be paying thousands of dollars each year in taxes alone, something many people don't consider when making their initial calculations.

Another major expense is closing costs. These can include bank fees, legal fees, inspection costs, and other administrative charges. While they may seem like small amounts individually, together they can add up to between 2% and 5% of the home's total price. This means that if you buy a $200,000 property, you could end up paying an additional $4,000 to $10,000 in these costs alone, and many buyers don't find out until they're about to sign the contract.

Repairs and maintenance are another aspect that many overlook. When you rent, any problems with the plumbing, roof, or appliances are the landlord's responsibility. But when you own the home, it all falls on you. Some homes require immediate repairs after purchase, and if you don't have an emergency fund for these unforeseen events, you could find yourself in a difficult financial situation. Even if you buy a new home, it's inevitable that maintenance expenses will arise over time, such as painting, landscaping improvements, changing locks, and other small details that add up more than you might think.

Homeowners insurance is another cost you can't ignore. Many people don't consider the impact this fee has on their monthly budget. Depending on the location and value of your home, you could be paying hundreds of dollars a month in insurance, and if the area is at risk for flooding, earthquakes, or other natural disasters, you may need additional coverage that further increases the cost.

If you buy a home in a gated community or apartment building, you'll likely have to pay maintenance or homeowners' association fees. These fees may include common area maintenance, security, and other services, but they can sometimes be surprisingly high. In some exclusive communities, these fees can reach several hundred dollars a month, directly impacting your ability to pay.

Another expense many people don't consider is the cost of utilities. If you're coming from a small apartment or living with relatives, you're probably not used to paying high electricity, water, gas, and internet bills. When you move to a larger home, these costs can double or even triple. Additionally, in some areas, you're required to pay for services like garbage collection or street maintenance, something that's often not mentioned at the time of purchase.

In addition to these costs, there are unexpected expenses that can arise over time. You may discover you need new furniture because the current ones don't fit in your new home, or you may need to upgrade your lighting, change locks for security, or even invest in curtains and appliances that weren't included in your purchase. All of these small details add up to thousands of dollars you hadn't considered at the outset.

A smart strategy to avoid surprises is to create a realistic budget from the start. Don't limit yourself to calculating just the mortgage and down payment, but consider all these additional costs to ensure you can really afford the home you want. It's also a good idea to have an emergency fund to cover any unexpected expenses that may arise after the purchase.

Many first-time buyers get so excited about owning their own home that they overlook these details, only to realize later that they're deeper in debt than they expected. Avoid falling into this trap and plan every aspect of the purchase well. Knowing the hidden costs in advance will allow you to make a better decision and enjoy your home without unnecessary worries.

From Offer to Contract

Making an offer on a home is an exciting time and, at the same time, one of the most critical stages of the home buying process. This is the step where you define how much you're willing to pay and the terms under which you wish to acquire the property. But what many people don't know is that making an offer is just the beginning of a series of negotiations that will culminate in the signing of a legally binding contract. If you're not clear on how this process works, you could end up committing to terms that aren't favorable to you or, worse yet, missing out on the opportunity to buy the home you want.

The first thing you should do before submitting an offer is assess the property's true value. Don't rely solely on the asking price, as it may be inflated or, in some cases, below market value. Research how much similar homes in the same area have sold for in recent months. This will give you an idea of whether the price is fair and help you determine how much you should offer. It's also a good idea to have your real estate agent conduct a comparative analysis to ensure you're making an informed decision.

Once you're clear on the property's value and how much you're willing to pay, it's time to write your offer. This document not only includes your asking price but also other important terms and conditions. These include specifying whether you want the seller to cover certain closing costs, including appliances, making certain repairs before the sale, and how much time you have to complete the inspection and secure financing. The more detailed your offer is, the less room there will be for confusion or misunderstandings in the future.

After presenting the offer, the seller has three options: accept it as is, reject it, or make a counteroffer. In most cases, the seller will attempt to negotiate, which means you must be prepared to respond quickly and strategically. This is where your negotiating skills come into play. If the seller counteroffers a higher price or different terms, you must evaluate whether you are willing to accept those terms or prefer to make another counteroffer. This exchange can continue until both parties reach an agreement or until one decides to withdraw from the negotiation.

When both parties finally agree to the terms, the offer becomes a sales contract. At this point, you'll need to deposit an amount of money known as an "earnest money deposit" or "good faith deposit." This money demonstrates your commitment to the purchase and, in most cases, will be applied to the down payment on the home. However, it's important to read the contract carefully to ensure there's a clause that allows you to recover this money if something goes wrong during the process, such as not obtaining financing or if the inspection reveals serious problems with the property.

Once the contract is signed, a due diligence phase begins, with inspections and appraisals to ensure the home is in good condition and worth what you're paying for it. This is where you may discover hidden problems that could make you reconsider the purchase or renegotiate the price. If the inspection reveals serious issues, you can ask the seller to repair them before closing or request a discount on the purchase price to cover the costs of the repairs.

Another crucial step in this phase is the property appraisal. If you're getting a mortgage, the bank will require an appraisal to ensure the house is worth what you're paying. If the appraisal comes in lower than the agreed-upon price, you'll have to renegotiate with the seller or cover the difference with your own money, which can be a problem if you don't have extra financial leeway.

It's also important to review all legal documents related to the property. Make sure there are no issues with the title, such as previous mortgages, outstanding debts, or legal disputes that could complicate the purchase. You can do this with the help of a specialized attorney or through a title company. Don't assume everything is in order just because the seller tells you so.

Finally, when all the conditions of the contract have been met and both you and the seller are ready to close the transaction, the signing of the deed is scheduled. At this point, you'll make the final payment, sign the legal documents, and receive the keys to your new home. Although it may seem like a long and complex process, each of these steps is essential to ensure a safe purchase and that you're making the best possible investment.

From the offer to the contract, every decision you make will impact the final outcome of the purchase. If you prepare well, negotiate wisely, and review every detail carefully, you'll have a much better chance of landing your dream home in the best possible conditions.

The Perfect Move

Moving into your new home is the final step in the homebuying process, but it's no less important. In fact, a poorly planned move can turn into a headache filled with stress, unforeseen events, and unnecessary expenses. To make sure everything goes smoothly, you need to organize every detail in advance and ensure the transition is as smooth as possible. A perfect move isn't a matter of luck, but rather strategy and preparation.

The first step is to set the exact date you'll be moving. Not all dates are the same. Weekends and the end of the month are typically the busiest days for moving companies, which can lead to higher prices and limited availability. If you're flexible, consider moving on less busy days, such as mid-month or during the week. Also, make sure the house will be ready for you on your chosen date. Sometimes, there may be delays in handing over keys or activating basic services like electricity, water, and internet, which could complicate your arrival.

Once you've set a date, the next step is to take a detailed inventory of all your belongings. You can't imagine how much stuff you've accumulated over time until it's time to pack it up. It's a good idea to take this opportunity to get rid of what you no longer need. You can sell, donate, or discard items you no longer use instead of lugging them to your new home. This will not only help you reduce the amount of moving, but will also make the unpacking process much easier and faster.

The next step is to pack strategically. Many people make the mistake of simply stuffing things into boxes haphazardly, which makes finding what you need in your new home a chaotic mess. The key is to pack by category and label each box carefully. Use sturdy boxes and be sure to protect fragile items with bubble wrap or blankets. Don't forget to create a special box for the essential items you'll need for the first few days, such as clothing, toiletries, chargers, important documents, and some kitchen utensils. This way, you won't have to open all the boxes looking for the basics while you settle in.

Now it's time to decide how you'll move. You have two main options: do it yourself or hire a professional service. If you decide to do it yourself, you'll need to secure a suitable vehicle, recruit friends or family to help, and make sure everything is properly packed to prevent damage. On the other hand, hiring a moving company can save you a lot of work and stress, although it does involve an additional cost. If you opt for a moving company, be sure to research different options, compare prices, and read reviews to choose one that is reliable and efficient. Also, ask if they offer insurance in case of damage or loss during the move.

Another key point is coordinating the connection of basic services in your new home. There's nothing worse than moving in and realizing you don't have electricity, water, or internet. It's best to schedule the activation of these services in advance so that everything is working from day one. Also, if you have subscriptions or important correspondence, remember to update your address with banks, utility companies, and any other institutions that send documents to your home.

On moving day, be sure to supervise the entire process and check that you haven't left anything behind in your old home. Do a final inspection of each room, closet, and drawer to make sure you haven't forgotten anything important. If you hired a moving company, check that all your belongings arrive in good condition and in the right place.

Once you arrive in your new home, don't rush into unpacking everything in one day. Start with the essentials and gradually organize each space functionally. Enjoy the process and take the time to adjust to your new surroundings.

Moving into your new home is an exciting experience, but it can become stressful if you're not well organized. With good planning, you can make the transition smoothly, avoiding unforeseen events and ensuring that your new home welcomes you with everything ready to begin this new stage of your life.

Your First Home as an Investment for the Future

Buying your first home doesn't just mean having a roof over your head and no longer paying rent; it can also be one of the best investments of your life if you make strategic decisions from the start. Many people view their home solely as a place to live, not realizing that, with good planning, that property can become a source of income or an asset that increases in value over time. Thinking of your home as an investment will allow you to get the most out of it and ensure that your purchase not only provides stability but also helps you build wealth in the future.

The first thing you need to understand is that the value of a property isn't fixed. Depending on the location, the development of the area, and market demand, your home can increase in value over the years. Therefore, choosing the right area to buy is key. It's not just about whether it's beautiful or comfortable, but also whether it has growth potential. Places close to new construction, commercial developments, or infrastructure improvements tend to increase in value more quickly. Research what projects are planned in the area and whether it's a growing area or an area where prices have remained stagnant.

Another key aspect is how you finance your home. If you manage to obtain a loan with a low interest rate and affordable monthly payments, you'll be able to keep your property without it becoming a financial burden. Furthermore, if you ever decide to sell it, well-structured financing will allow you to do so without the interest costs having significantly affected your profit.

But it's not just about selling in the future; there are many ways to make money from your first home while you're still using it. One of the most popular strategies is renting out part of the property. If you buy a house with more than one room, or even a separate space, you could rent it out to someone else and thereby reduce your own housing costs. Many people have paid their mortgage by renting out a room or a small apartment within their property.

Another option is to consider short-term rental platforms like Airbnb. If your home is located in a tourist area or a high-demand area, you could take advantage of this option to generate extra income when you're not using the property. Even if you live there, you could rent out a space during specific periods and make money without significantly impacting your lifestyle.

Home maintenance is also an important part of its investment value. A well-maintained property with constant improvements appreciates more quickly than one left to deteriorate over time. Making small renovations, upgrading finishes, and keeping it in good condition will not only make your home more pleasant to live in, but will also increase its value if you ever decide to sell or rent it.

If after a while you decide you want to buy another home, you could turn your first property into a long-term investment. Instead of selling it, you could keep it as a rental property and use the income from that property to pay for the new one. This is how many people get started in the real estate world, making their first home the starting point for building a property portfolio.

Viewing your home as an investment from the start will allow you to make better decisions and maximize its potential. You're not just buying a place to live, but an asset that can grow in value, generate income, and open up financial opportunities in the future. Thinking strategically and planning with a long-term vision can ensure your first home isn't just an expense, but the foundation of your financial stability and a tool for building wealth over time.

www.ingramcontent.com/pod-product-compliance
Lightning Source LLC
LaVergne TN
LVHW090425210926
848480LV00002B/695

* 9 7 9 8 2 2 7 7 3 9 9 7 1 *